Up-Grade!

Light relief between grades

Pamela Wedgwood

Spaß und Entspannung mit leichten Originalstücken für Flöte
Erster Schwierigkeitsgrad

Plaisir et détente avec des pièces originales simples pour flûte
Niveau 1

FABER *ff* MUSIC

Foreword

Up-Grade! is a collection of new pieces and duets in a wide variety of styles for flautists of any age. This book is designed to be especially useful to students who have passed Grade 1 and would like a break before plunging into the syllabus for Grade 2.

Whether you're looking for stimulating material to help bridge the gap between grades, or simply need a bit of light relief, I hope you'll enjoy *Up-Grade!*

Pamela Wedgwood

This collection © 1998 by Faber Music Ltd
First published in 1998 by Faber Music Ltd
3 Queen Square London WC1N 3AU
Cover illustration by John Levers
Cover design by S & M Tucker
Music processed by Jackie Leigh
Printed in England by Halstan & Co Ltd
All rights reserved

ISBN 0 571 51818 4

To buy Faber Music publications or to find out about the full range of titles available please contact your local retailer or Faber Music sales enquiries:

Tel: +44 (0)171 833 7931
Fax: +44 (0)171 278 3817
E-mail: sales@fabermusic.co.uk
Website: http://www.fabermusic.co.uk

CONTENTS

1.   Take It Easy   *Pamela Wedgwood*   4

2.   Land of Hope and Glory   *Edward Elgar*   4

3.   Apple Pie Waltz   *Pamela Wedgwood*   5

4.   Banana Boat Song   *Traditional*   5

5.   What shall we do with the Drunken Sailor?   *Traditional*   6

6.   La Donna e Mobile   *Giuseppe Verdi*   6

7.   Rosemary and Thyme   *Pamela Wedgwood*   7

8.   Greensleeves   *attrib. Henry VIII*   7

9.   Can Can   *Jacques Offenbach*   8

10.   The Contented Frog   *Pamela Wedgwood*   8

11.   Theme from 'The Teddy Bears' Picnic'   *J.W. Bratton*   9

12.   Off to the Sun   *Pamela Wedgwood*   9

13.   Chinese Take It Away   *Pamela Wedgwood*   10

14.   It's Duet Time! (two duets in A minor)   *Pamela Wedgwood*   10

15.   Fandango (a duet)   *Pamela Wedgwood*   12

1. Take It Easy

Pamela Wedgwood

2. Land of Hope and Glory

Edward Elgar

3. Apple Pie Waltz

Pamela Wedgwood

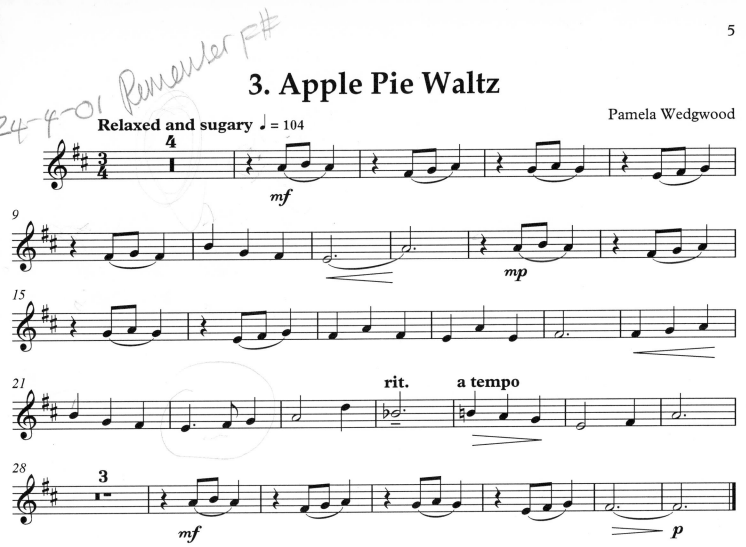

4. Banana Boat Song

Traditional

5. What shall we do with the Drunken Sailor?

As fast as possible

Traditional

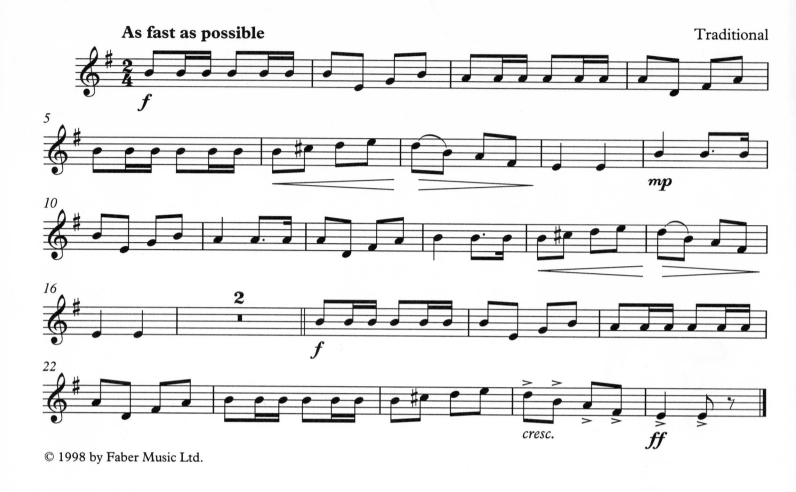

6. La Donna e Mobile

Allegretto ♩ = 120

Giuseppe Verdi

7. Rosemary and Thyme

Pamela Wedgwood

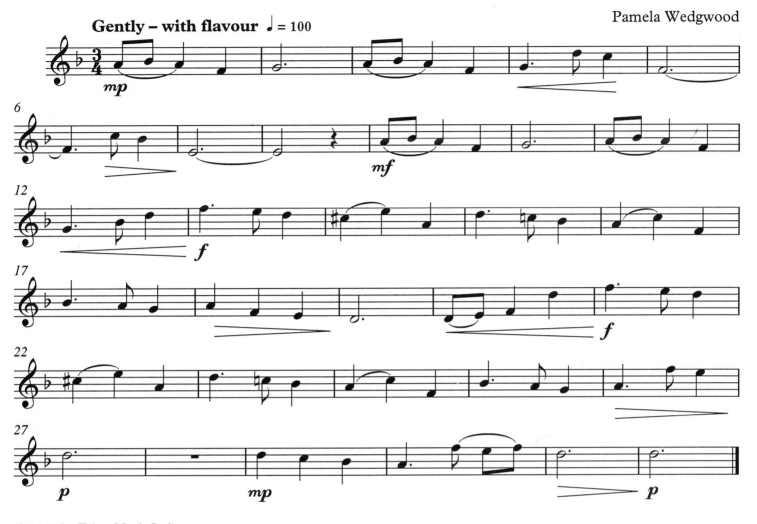

8. Greensleeves

attrib. Henry VIII

8

9. Can Can

Jacques Offenbach

10. The Contented Frog

Pamela Wedgwood

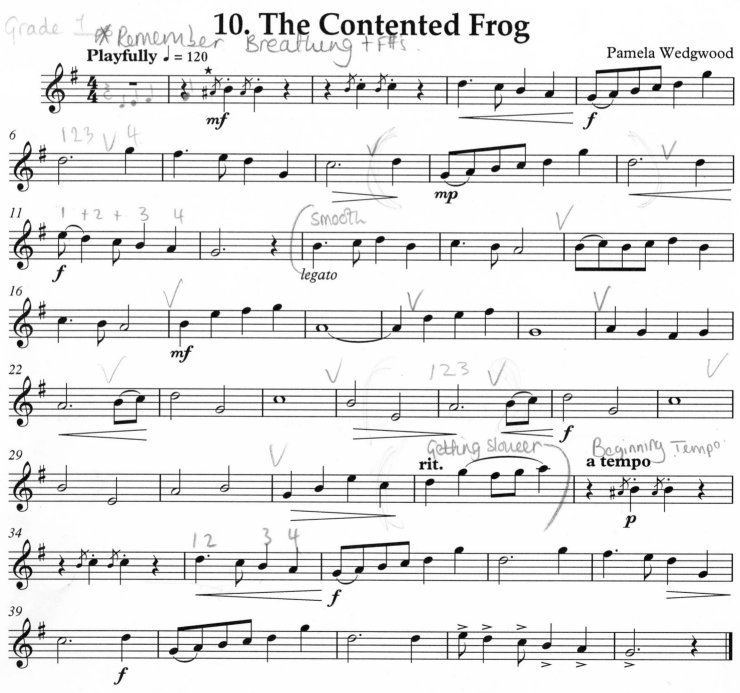

* Use alternative fingering for A♯

11. Theme from 'The Teddy Bears' Picnic'

J.W. Bratton

12. Off to the Sun

Pamela Wedgwood

13. Chinese Take It Away

14. It's Duet Time!

two duets in A minor

Pamela Wedgwood

② **In march time** ♩ = 116

Instrument 1

Instrument 2

15. Fandango (a duet)

Pamela Wedgwood